S is for Ska

by
Geoff Munn

S is for Ska

Published by The Brothers Uber

To our Kickstarter backers,
you all made this happen.

Aa

americana

Bb

bluegrass

Dd

dubstep

Ee

emo

Ff

funk

Gg

grunge

Hh

hip hop

Ii

industrial

Jj

jazz

Kk

k-pop

Ll

latin

Mm

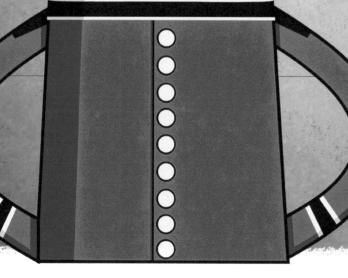

muzak

Nn

nerdcore

Oo

opera

Pp

pop

Qq

quartet (barbershop)

Rr

reggae

Ss

ska (3rd wave)

Tt

techno

Uu

urban folk

Vv

video game

Ww

world

Xx

xoomii

Yy

yodeling

Zz

zydeco

About the Illustrator:

Geoff Munn

Geoff was born in 1978 in Elmira, NY. Always armed with a passion to draw and an overactive imagination, he continued to develop his skills and migrated to Pittsburgh, PA, where he graduated from The Art Institute of Pittsburgh. As a digital artist, Geoff has had the pleasure of working for video game companies, contributing art and animation to games from Disney, Cartoon Network, Marvel Comics, and Children's Workshop. He has also been featured as a sketch artist for Lucasfilm on trading cards from Topps, and has helped several companies develop animated TV pilots, brand identities, and with other art assets.

Currently living in Pittsburgh, PA with his wife and son, Geoff works as a freelance artist/illustrator. In his spare time, he creates several webcomics and independent animated films. While working digitally is his main focus, Geoff also works traditionally, and has been developing his painting skills on the side.

CPSIA information can be obtained
at www.ICGtesting.com
Printed in the USA
BVHW020914300919
559784BV00014B/555/P